Old POLLOKSHAWS

by

George Rountree

The infant class, Pollok Academy, 1883. Elizabeth Mitchell is sitting fifth from the left in the middle row.

© George Rountree 2002
First published in the United Kingdom, 2002,
by Stenlake Publishing
Telephone / Fax: 01290 551122

ISBN 1 84033 220 4

The author's royalties from the sale of this book have been donated to the Prince and Princess of Wales Hospice.

ACKNOWLEDGEMENTS

The author would like to thank the following people and organisations for providing pictures and information: George Smith; members of Pollokshaws Heritage, in particular Anna Simpson who supplied a copy of the Pollokshaws Compulsory Purchase Order, 1959; Gavin Stamp; Hugh McKenzie who provided the photograph of his late uncle, also Hugh McKenzie; and Bob Collins. Many of the pictures in this book, including those on the cover, were taken by Nettie Wren during the 1960s. Her foresight in photographing the area during this period has created an invaluable record of Pollokshaws prior to its redevelopment, and she deserves special thanks.

The publishers would like to thank George Heaney for making available slides from his collection showing Pollokshaws in the 1950s. These were copied during the 1980s from photographs held by the Planning Department of Glasgow City Council. We are grateful to Steve Hosey of Development and Regeneration Services at the City Council for permission to use the slides. Thanks are also due to Robert Grieves for providing the picture on page 41; the staff of the National Library of Scotland Map Library; and Mrs Helen Simpson who provided the class photograph on page 1 which includes her mother. Special thanks are due to Dr Anne Loudon, co-author of *Old Newton Mearns*, who put the author in touch with the publishers and provided valuable help in gathering additional material for this book.

FURTHER READING

The books listed below were used by the author during his research. None of them are available from Stenlake Publishing. Those interested in finding out more are advised to contact their local bookshop or reference library.

Auldfield Parish Church, *History 1764–1959*
Blair, Anna, *Tea at Miss Cranston's* (omnibus), 1998
Galt, John, *The Entail*, 1820, reprinted 1984 (the author refers to Pollokshaws as Camrachle)
Hume, John R., *The Industrial Archaeology of Glasgow*, 1974.
McCallum, Andrew, *Pollokshaws, Village and Burgh, 1600–1912*, 1925
McDonald, Hugh, *Rambles Round Glasgow*, 1854, reprinted 1910
Smart, Aileen, *Villages of Glasgow Vol. II*, 1996
Watson, Robert, *Stranger than his Sea*, c.1900 (the author refers to Pollokshaws as Piershaws)
Watson, Robert, *The Native Returns*, 1932 (unpublished)
Williams, Riches & Higgs, *The Buildings of Scotland – Glasgow*, 1990
Wingate, Dr Guy A. S., *Born to Coal, The History of the Wingate Family* (unpublished)

INTRODUCTION

In the sixteenth century a meal mill was built by the then Laird of Pollok on the banks of the River Cart at the Shaw Bridge, which his tenant farmers were required to use. This was one of the first important landmarks in what was to become Pollokshaws. The fledgling village was situated at the crossing point of two important roads; one between Glasgow and Irvine, the other linking Govan with Cathcart and Rutherglen. From the time of the Industrial Revolution until the middle of the twentieth century, the 'Shaws grew to become a hive of industrial activity, initially taking advantage of the water power that the original meal mill depended on. At first involved in cloth manufacturing and bleaching, Pollokshaws expanded into cotton thread manufacturing, leather processing, pottery and paper making, ironfounding, boiler making and engineering.

Many of these new industries required a dependable supply of clean water, so the mill lade was constructed around 1800 by the prominent industrialist Archibald Ingram (the weir had been built at the same time as the meal mill in order to increase water power to the mill). Using the bed of the Auldhouse Burn, which up to that time joined the River Cart close to where the Pollokshaws Road bridge stands today, the lade flowed from a point behind what later became Harriet Street, past the rear of where Shawbridge Street south of river is today before turning west to pass under it. The main flow of the burn was diverted through what is now Auldhouse Park and into the River Cart above the weir.

Like other Scottish towns with similar origins, Pollokshaws grew in an erratic way with streets at odd angles to one another and seemingly random rows of buildings of different heights in close proximity. Thus there was a mixture of early ground floor, one- and two-storey buildings, which were joined up later with single and two-close three-storey buildings. Latterly there were blocks of tenements constructed like those seen elsewhere around Glasgow, all of which combined to produce a streetscape of irregular but interesting outline.

Pollokshaws became a burgh of barony in 1812 (at which time its population was almost 3,000), and in 1898 Sir John Maxwell built and gifted the Burgh Halls to the town at a cost to himself of £20,000. The halls provided a large community meeting place and have served many purposes over the years. Following a hiatus a few years ago when Glasgow City Council proposed their closure, the halls were transferred into the hands of a trust.

The arrival of the Glasgow, Barrhead & Neilston Railway in 1849, the trams in the 1880s and the Cathcart Circle line of the Caledonian Railway Company in 1894 (electrified in 1962) helped boost expansion of industry and improve the mobility of the population.

Around 1890 Cowglen Fever Hospital was constructed, housed in a wooden building on a small plot of ground on the south side of Cowglen (now Barrhead) Road, about a quarter of a mile west of the Round Toll. Following the First World War the former hospital building was occupied by Howat, the local blacksmith turned farmer, and was known as Bangorshill Farm. In 1893 the Burgh co-operated with Barrhead and the Eastern District Committee of Renfrewshire to establish Darnley Hospital. In the following year Pollokshaws District Nursing Association was set up.

During the 1950s the population of Pollokshaws stood at around 100,000, a figure which included the newly-developed adjacent areas of Auldhouse, Mansewood and Eastwood. At this time rumours were circulating that radical changes were on the way, along the lines of those planned for certain other districts of the city. These were to culminate in the far-reaching redevelopment schemes of the 1960s. The replacement of the trams with buses in 1958 on the routes which served Pollokshaws foreshadowed the more major changes that were to come, and within a year the first significant upheaval in the town was caused by the lifting of the tram tracks.

Pollok Estate has always been integrally linked to the 'Shaws and when the Burrell Collection found a home there in 1983 there was some resentment among locals, because it meant the loss of part of one of the largest grassy areas in the estate to which the public had access. But the remarkable building which was built to house the collection, and the sense almost that it 'belonged' to the 'Shaws, has since made people regard the museum as a major asset. It was the end of an era when in 1969, after a family association of nearly 700 years, the Freedom of the City of Glasgow 'in recognition of her family's many benefactions and long service to the people of Pollokshaws' was conferred on Mrs Anne Maxwell Macdonald, daughter of the last Laird, Sir John Stirling Maxwell, following her donation of Pollok House and Estate to Glasgow City Council.

Between 1945 and 1959 I worked for the Pollokshaws Co-operative Society, and although mainly employed in branches outwith Pollokshaws, I got to know the town a little. After marrying a Pollokshaws girl and coming here to live in 1958, I became better acquainted with the burgh's character and learned a little of its origins. Retirement in 1983 meant there was time to conduct research into my family history, which expanded to become an interest in local history. Through time, having collected some old prints and other more recent images, as well as having read all I could find about the history of Pollokshaws, I felt the time had come for a book of photographs to be produced. As far as possible the pictures have been arranged in sequence as a walk round the old burgh – I hope you enjoy the journey.

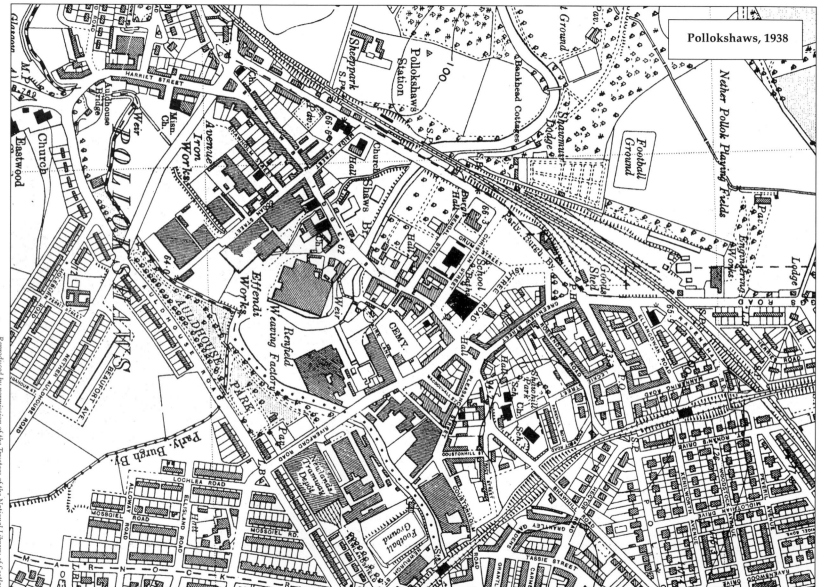

Pollokshaws, 1938

This photograph shows Whins of Potterfield, a hamlet which was situated in Haggs Road at Whins Road. Miners who worked in Lochinch pit (located on what is now the site of the riding school off Dumbreck Road) lived here, and about six of their children are visible in the picture, if rather indistinctly. The distant feature on the extreme left could be the houses with heavy mullions in Moray Place, Strathbungo, designed by Alexander 'Greek' Thomson and built in 1858. On the right, rising above the railway line, is North Hill where Ravenshall Road and Mannering Road lie today and which continues on to become High Shawlands. The villas on North Hill date from the late 1890s so this photograph must have been taken between 1858 and the latter date. Nearby Shawmoss Road is named after the farm of the same name; its farmhouse still exists as a well-kept private dwelling. For many years Crossmyloof ice rink occupied what is now the Safeway site, and the adjacent area of new housing alongside the railway, which dates from the 1980s, was allotment gardens.

Haggs Road in 1928 looking north, with the LMS Railway's Pollokshaws North signal box on the left behind the lantern of the gas lamp. There was a railway goods yard in the area on the left above the sleeper fence, which is now occupied by a car showroom. At one time the yard spanned both sides of the line as far as the lane giving access to Bankhead allotments. Haggs Road railway bridge was replaced and the road widened in 1930. The building partly visible on the right, an electricity sub-station, was built by Glasgow Corporation Electricity Department in 1908. Leading off to the right before the bridge is Ravenshall Road. The hamlet of Whins of Potterfield stood a few hundred yards beyond the bridge.

Pollokshaws Road from opposite the Burgh Halls, *c*.1957. The first wartime emergency fire station in the area was set up in the Sir John Maxwell School in 1939. In 1941 temporary fire station buildings were erected on ground next to Wellgreen known as Craigies Park (now the site of Wellgreen Court); they are the low white buildings seen on the left of this picture. During the war the service was known as the AFS (Auxiliary Fire Service) and the code of this station was 3CZ; after the war ended the name changed to the NFS (National Fire Service). When the new fire station opened in Brockburn Road, Pollok, in the 1950s, this one was closed. The buildings in the background on the left are in Greenview Street at Pollokshaws Road. The gable with the two advertising posters on it is in Wellgreen, with the roof of the tenement known as the Bank building behind and above it. On the skyline are St Conval's Primary School and the round 'witch's hat' tower of the Infants' School.

Shawmuir Lodge on Pollok Avenue, photographed in 1961. Nettie Wren, the principal contributor of photographs to this book, is seen here with her cousin Jenny Sharp (right) who lived in the lodge as a tenant at this time. The original avenue between Pollok House and Pollokshaws Road at Haggs Road ran in an almost straight line, but the building of the railway at its eastern end in the 1840s led to the last quarter mile being diverted to emerge from under the railway beside the River Cart at what was then Barrhead Road (now Pollokshaws Road). A section of the abandoned avenue can still be seen, magnificently lined with mature trees, behind Bankhead allotments. The realigned avenue is one of two main approaches to Pollok House and the Burrell Collection. An interesting feature nearby is the remains of a pedestrian suspension bridge. A concrete plinth and steel stanchions can be seen on both banks of the River Cart from the riverside walk in Pollok Estate close to the tennis courts. It is likely that the bridge was installed for the convenience of city- or estate-bound workers arriving at Pollokshaws West railway station when it and the railway viaduct over the river were constructed in 1847. At that time estate workers probably numbered around 50. The bridge was in use up until the Second World War, but was dismantled not long afterwards. Its remains are well concealed among the greenery and are best seen in winter.

When the bridge carrying Pollokshaws Road over the River Cart was widened in 1930 trams had to be provided with a temporary track and overhead power supply, as illustrated here. There only appears to have been a single line of track, and consequently this would have carried traffic in both directions, probably at a severely restricted speed. The upstream section of the bridge (seen here) would have been built first to carry the track while the old bridge was demolished. But what about pedestrians? Were they expected to walk along the loose kerbstones? The house nearby at the corner of Pollok Avenue was owned by Nether Pollok Ltd. and occupied by Ernest Pickwell. He and his son John are reputed to have owned the area of land between Bengal Street and the river known as the Orchard, and are listed as owning the garage at 130 Shawbridge Street, which overlooked the river at the Shaw Bridge. Its forecourt was situated high above the river and there were lockups which backed on to it.

This photograph of an accident at Pollokshaws West station was printed from a frame of newsreel footage dating from 1925 or 1926. The Caley Jumbo engine had been shunting in the main 'up' (east) goods yard and had drawn up to the exit signal with its train to await clearance onto the main line. When the signal for the main line was drawn 'off', giving clearance for another train approaching, the Jumbo driver thought it was for him and started up. Engine and train ran into the headshunt, went through the buffer stops and demolished the signal box, which at that time was on the east side of the line. They then rolled down the embankment and finished up in the garden of the Pickwells' house. This scene of the recovery of the engine

presents a mystery, as it appears to have been taken at Pollokshaws West station which is on the opposite side of the river from where the train landed. The only features visible here that could identify the location, other than the signals, are the barely discernible curve of the stonework arch of the bridge and a buttress at the entrance to Pollok Estate at 2060 Pollokshaws Road. These are in line with the left-hand corner of the engine cab roof.

10

Pollokshaws Road at Maida Street, 1961. Until 1930 the stretch of Pollokshaws Road between Haggs Road and what is known locally as The West (the Round Toll) was called Barrhead Road, while the present Barrhead Road was called Cowglen Road. (Pollokshaws Road's continuation from Haggs Road to the Cathcart Circle railway bridge at Shawlands station was called Maxwell Street.) Pollok United Free Church (1848), later Pollok Church of Scotland, seen on the right of this picture, stood at the corner of Maida Street. It was demolished some time after completion of the main redevelopment scheme in the late 1960s, after which sheltered housing for Kirk Care was built on the site. The stone gateway pillars seen here remain, and having been realigned flank pedestrian access to the adjacent housing area and the Kirk Care flats. At the far right-hand edge of the picture is the corner of Pollok Academy, which was built in 1856 and stood on the other corner of Maida Street.

Sir John Maxwell Bt. was a major contributor of funds towards Pollok Academy (1856), the last school to be built in Pollokshaws before the introduction of the Education Act of 1872. The partnership of Baird & Thomson, comprising Sir John's own architect John Baird II and the latter's brother-in-law Alexander 'Greek' Thomson, was responsible for its design. It is not clear which of the two architects contributed which elements of the building, but it has been suggested that the gable windows, grouped unusually in threes, reflect the style of Alexander Thomson, as do the chimneys. The section on the right including the clock tower formed the original school, while the rest of the building, by Baird alone, was added in 1874/75 after ownership had passed to Eastwood Parish School Board. An arcaded corridor was used to connect the two parts of the building. The basement was in two sections on the same level as the playground, one part in the original building and the other in the extension. These areas were used as shelters for pupils when the weather was bad.

Glimpsed on the left through the railway arch in 1961, Sheeppark Lodge, like all the other buildings seen here, was soon to be a casualty of the redevelopment. It was one of several smaller buildings within and around the perimeter of the Pollok Estate which were occupied by estate workers and their families. The road through the arch leads to Pollokshaws Bowling Club (1854), which lies on the photographer's right, the greens of which until the mid-1950s were situated in the area visible on the far side of Pollokshaws Road beyond the remaining Lodge stone gate pillars. Sheeppark Farm lies farther up the road behind the camera. Beyond the former farm buildings, now dwellings, it becomes a secluded footpath which continues on past Pollok golf course to Pollok House and is frequented by walkers and cyclists. Near the end of the track, at the foot of a tree-covered eminence on the right and close to the river, there is a flat, square, rather muddy area which is the site of the former estate curling pond. Construction of Pollok House commenced in 1747 and the building was completed in 1752; at the time it was described as 'a small but genteel box'. It was extended between 1890 and 1908 by the 10th Baronet, Sir John Stirling-Maxwell, to a design by his then architect Robert Rowand Anderson (along with the latter's partner, A. F. Balfour Paul). It was in the Cedar Room at Pollok House that discussions leading to the formation of the NTS in 1931 took place.

The Round Toll, *c*.1910. This view looks up Cartcraigs (later Kennishead) Road from near the original Methodist Church (built 1883). At the top of the hill the road crossed the railway by a bridge which today is a footbridge. Beyond the bridge Cartcraigs Road was a quiet country road with a reputation as a lovers' lane. Within the area of this view there was once a school, Eastwood Academy, marked on Richardson's map dated 1796, to which men who had gone overseas to Jamaica as planters sent their children to be educated. Standing near the site of the present multi-storey building, it became known as the black boys' school. Howat's smiddy occupied the low building on the right and there was another forge across the road, Cunningham's, the entrance to which was situated by the pole on the right. The present alignment of Barrhead Road/Kennishead Road was laid out in the mid-1960s.

The Round Toll house dates from about 1800 and this view from Barrhead Road was taken *c*.1957. Road tolls were introduced in 1750 and abolished in 1883, after which the tollhouse was used for other purposes. Another similar but earlier photograph shows it with a sign reading: 'George Smith, Carriage Hirer, Telephones: National: 54X4, Corp: ZO425, House: Corp ZO426'. At that time there were two telephone services in the Glasgow area, one operated by the National Telephone Company and the other by Glasgow Corporation. The building was used as a dwelling for a time but eventually became vacant. It was restored in 1973 but now stands isolated on the traffic roundabout at what has always been known locally as 'The West'. From the left are Cunningham's garage, the original Methodist Church (1883), the Jubilee building and the Round Toll house.

This photograph of Barrhead Road and Broomhill Farm dates from *c.*1950. The location is about 200 yards east of Boydstone Road, and today the farmhouse (left) is a crumbling ruin. The dual carriageway, which was built in 1938, ran immediately past the front door, swallowing up the farm's garden. Here the impression is of much effort having been put into making the steading look smart, with the ricks – corn to the front and larger ones of hay at the back – seemingly built with architectural precision. As a bus driver in the 1960s I remember having to occasionally draw up to allow cattle to cross the dual carriageway between the estate and the farmyard.

This photograph shows Broomhill Farm in the early 1930s. The garden in the foreground was subsequently buried under the dual carriageway, something that farmer John Smith may have been anticipating when the picture was taken. Older people will remember an unusual building long since demolished which stood on land belonging to Broomhill Farm. It was situated to the east of Boydstone Road, a few hundred yards from its junction with Barrhead Road. An old stone-built structure covered with ivy and standing a few yards back from the road, it was known as the Ivy Castle (on the 1913 OS map it is marked as 'Ivy Tower'). About the size of a villa, its curious location was compounded by its odd appearance, as it had a flat roof. However, the OS map of 1858 gives a clue as to its original use, labelling it as 'engine house'. Mining was carried out in this area during the nineteenth century and where required coal-fired steam-driven pumping engines were set up to extract water from mine workings. They were usually regarded as long-term fixtures needing protection, so substantial buildings were put up to house them. When mining ceased in the area around the 1900s and the pump was no longer required, the building was converted into houses and two families lived there.

Looking down Pollokshaws Road from the Round Toll in 1961 to the Afton Terrace tenement and its gable covered with advertising posters. On the right is the corner of the original Pollokshaws Methodist Church and in the distance Pollok Academy can be seen with its clock tower. There were a number of buildings to the left along the foot of the railway embankment, most of which were dwellings, although one was the hall of the Orange Lodge which – as part of the redevelopment – had to move to premises near the Shaw Bridge. Another was a house which was occupied by a provost, outside which an elderly resident remembers seeing two decorative provosts' lamp-posts at the pavement edge. The roughcast structure at the back edge of the pavement between the church and Afton Terrace was a gents' toilet. Within a few years all the buildings described were demolished for road widening, with the exception of Afton Terrace.

Cross Street and the rear of the Jubilee building, 1961. For many years there was a chip shop with seating accommodation here called the Jubilee Restaurant, and the building, with a truncated V ground plan, was know by the restaurant's name until it was demolished. Here the former chip shop premises at 2 Harriet Street are occupied by Thomas E. Smith & Sons Ltd., painters and decorators. However, there is something else of interest in the picture. Painted on the wall in large letters behind the woman in the centre, but only just visible, the EWS sign dates from the Second World War. Comprising yellow letters with black borders, it was one of a number seen in built-up areas that were not near to rivers or burns, the last such sign surviving until the late 1980s. At the height of the blitz, when incendiary bombs were being dropped, there were fears that the mains water supply would be insufficient to cope with a large number of fires. Additionally, in some cases HE (high explosive) bomb damage meant that mains water was not available. To fight fires reservoir tanks were built on vacant ground at strategic locations, thus providing an emergency water supply (EWS). The signs included an arrow below the letters, and the capacity of the tank was also usually shown. In this case the arrow points to the left to where the tank stood on a vacant site behind the Methodist Church. The tanks were assembled from three-foot-square pressed steel flanged sections which could be bolted together to form containers of various capacities. At first the tops were open, but drowning incidents made a wire mesh covering necessary. The tanks became attractive to children because after a year or so without being used they became a habitat for wildlife, including minnows, while there was the more obvious hazard of swimming in warm weather. The three-inch-deep flanges on the outside allowed curious youngsters, of which I was one, to climb up the sides.

The tram terminus in Nether Auldhouse Road, photographed in the 1950s. Near here in Shawholm Street, John Dalglish founded (c.1874) the Avenue ironworks, specialising in the manufacture of textile finishing machinery, and in 1898/99 A. & W. Dalglish erected the West of Scotland Boiler Works in the same vicinity. Pollokshaws West's original tram terminus was a track crossover at the Methodist Church in Pollokshaws Road which was

Picture reproduced from STTS Collection

in use from 1902 to 1912. In that year the track was extended to Rouken Glen, although the 'West' terminus continued to be used regularly. As time passed traffic levels increased and the manoeuvre over the crossover became more and more hazardous. After the end of World War II it was decided to reduce the danger by making a double junction in Cross Street and laying out a terminus in quieter Nether Auldhouse Road (illustrated here). With a Corporation inspector, a policeman and others looking on, the arrival of Coronation tram 1211 on service 14 may have marked an unusual event. The Fischer current collector on the roof is still in the 'arrival' position, but the screens are being changed by the conductress to the destination on the other side of the city. This was in fact 'University', although the destination 'Lambhill via Charing Cross' has been caught on camera as it passed the display aperture. The current collector was pulled over by the cord seen hanging down over the upper deck front window.

Harriet Street looking south *c*.1910. A sign below the crossbar of the gas lamp standard on the left reads, 'Do not spit on the pavement' and what look like birds against the sky are the tram overhead electric span wire insulators. The lower buildings behind the lamp with the 'Do not spit' sign were removed in 1932 when Nether Auldhouse Road was laid out. Those with smoking chimneys in the distance were replaced by the present red sandstone council tenement at the corner of Westwood Road and Thornliebank Road.

Inset: The premises of James MacDougall, tailor and clothier, are just visible in the extreme right foreground of the main picture, at the corner of the Jubilee building. Mr MacDougall was provost of Pollokshaws between 1905 and 1911.

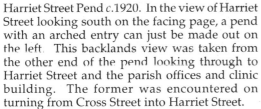

Harriet Street Pend c.1920. In the view of Harriet Street looking south on the facing page, a pend with an arched entry can just be made out on the left. This backlands view was taken from the other end of the pend looking through to Harriet Street and the parish offices and clinic building. The former was encountered on turning from Cross Street into Harriet Street.

Harriet Street in the 1950s looking north from opposite Wellmeadow Road and the Wellmeadow laundry (now Sunlight laundry). Harriet Street was narrow and the tramlines were laid close to the pavement on the left. Behind and to the left of the Bedford half-ton van is the Jubilee building.

Harriet Street from Wellmeadow Road, 1961. This picture shows the central stretch of Harriet Street in what is now part of Thornliebank Road. Bob McKay was the manager of the Co-op grocery shop (on the right) at this time. Greenbank Street, situated between the shop sunblinds on the right, was a short street with one close each side and a mission hall (now a children's clinic) on the left at the end. Beyond the end of the street there was a footbridge over the mill lade into Greenbank Park. The premises of Robert Blair, undertaker, were situated on the far corner of Greenbank Street in Harriet Street; the blue fronted double shop of Gavin Ramsay, ladies' and gents' outfitters, was on the far side, followed by a row of four shops with tiled frontages belonging to the Glasgow South (formerly Pollokshaws) Co-operative Society Ltd. The gable in the distance with posters on it is at Nether Auldhouse Road. Parked facing the camera is a Ford Consul with a 1953 registration number. Behind are a Hillman Minx and a Morris Minor, while the bus is a Leyland PD2/24 on the 45 service. The only protection that shopfronts needed when the photograph was taken were the iron concertina fold-along gates seen here covering the doorways.

Harriet Street from Westwood Road, 1961. The junction of Wellmeadow Road is on the left. Also on the left but out of sight are the former Wellmeadow laundry premises. In the foreground is an Austin Devon van conversion, while in the distance the Jubilee tenement can be seen. Harriet Street narrowed here and the road level was raised for the tram tracks, leading to the unusual situation of the pavement being lower than the road. Because of the narrowness of the street, problems were sometimes caused by drivers, especially carters, parking at the pavement edge and blocking the trams. The distance between the wheels on most carts was the same as that between the tram rails. This led to a ploy whereby on cobbled streets – where the steel-shod cartwheels made for a very uncomfortable and noisy ride – carters took every opportunity to steer onto the tram track, remaining on it for as long as possible. This went as far as defying a tram driver who was approaching from behind and who had a timetable to keep to.

Harriet Street north of Cross Street *c.*1962 at the point where it joined Shawbridge Street, with the first (unfinished) multi-storey flat at 93 Shawholm Crescent and a new low rise tenement building facing the rear of Afton Terrace. The shadow in the left foreground is that of the Jubilee building. The Old Coach Inn stood at 1 Harriet Street and James Pollok's shop occupied No. 3. The original Shawbridge Street ran in a relatively straight line between Maida Street and Cross Street, but subsequent realignment meant that its southern end joined Nether Auldhouse Road about 70 yards east of the old junction, at the point where Shawholm Street used to be. Harriet Street completely disappeared in the redevelopment.

Looking north from behind the Clachan Bar in Shawbridge Street, 1961. Below the church and the church hall, behind the wall on the far left in what was the playground of Pollok Academy, two huts can just be made out. Having been disused for a number of years, the academy was demolished soon after this, and here it looks as if the contractor is setting up to start work on it. Behind is Pollok Parish Church and hall; the name 'Dykes' church which was sometimes applied to it referred to a minister of the 1900s. In line with the Burgh Halls, an empty prefab in Maida Street is ready for demolition, and the Sir John Maxwell Primary School can be glimpsed centre right.

Shawbridge Street, 1961. On the right are the premises of Peter Scott, jeweller and watchmaker, followed by a store belonging to Adam Millar & Son, plumbers, at 243 Shawbridge Street. The extremely good quality two-storey building set back from the pavement (in Glasgow parlance the ground floor, containing shops, was not counted as one of the storeys) should never have been demolished, for its condition was similar to that of other tenements that were retained. However, if it had been spared its position today would be at the pavement edge between the police station and the multi-storey building at 215 Shawbridge Street! The foundations of Mrs Law's recently demolished prefab are visible in the gap site, while one of the shops behind the Volkswagen van is Tommy Doig's general store at No. 217. Glimpsed at the left-hand edge of the tenement referred to above is the rear of one in Cogan Street.

Shawbridge Street, 1961. To the left of centre is the sunlit face of what may then have been the oldest surviving tenement in the 'Shaws, the Royal George. It was reputedly built as a hotel in the days of the stagecoaches, and was the terminus of the Royal George coach service from the city, as well as a stopping point for other coaches passing through the burgh during the nineteenth century. The short spire and tower just visible on the right belonged to Auldfield Parish Church; the UF Church was on the same stretch of the street but set back out of sight. Between the churches there was a tenement block at 175 Shawbridge Street which was used as offices by John McDonald & Co. (pneumatic tools) Ltd., whose works premises were opposite at No. 194. Another nearby company which was in a related line of business to McDonald & Co. was Compressor Services Ltd. at 200 Shawbridge Street. The designation Maxwell Cross, seen on the corner of the Railway Vaults pub (right), must have long passed out of use, or was perhaps the invention of the publican or a signwriter. I cannot recall ever having heard it used, and extensive enquiries among older locals found only one or two who 'thought they remembered it'!

This letter, dated 8 October 1925, was sent to Anna (Anaple) Jenkins Sclater of 8 Ettrick Place, Newlands, Glasgow, by her cousin Ellen Muir Glanville. Ellen was the granddaughter of two members of the Pollokshaws United Original Secession Church, John Dick and Helen Muir, who had emigrated to New Zealand in 1863.

The Revd James Milne Smith was appointed as the first minister of the church in 1842, and his congregation moved into their permanent church building (the present Pollokshaws Parish Church, Shawbridge Street) on 6 November 1843. On 20 June 1863, under his leadership, about eleven families connected with the church embarked at London for New Zealand on the *Ganges*, an American clipper of 1,211 tons (in preparation for the move, Mr Smith had already made this arduous journey once before). After sixteen weeks at sea, the *Ganges* dropped anchor in Auckland on 12 October 1863 and began disembarking the next day, following inspections by customs and medical officials. Lloyd Walker, author of *The Faraway Land*, wrote 'None were more pleased [to arrive] than the immigrants from Pollokshaws, most of whom had only known the streets of Glasgow. As soon as they reached the shore, they gathered in a group, the Precentor struck the note and with full hearts they sang the Second Paraphrase.'

At the time the New Zealand government offered 40 acres of land free to immigrants over the age of twenty, and twenty acres to those under that age, providing the voyage had been made at the immigrants' expense. However, life on the Manukau Peninsula south-west of Auckland proved very hard. The soil was poor and in 1866–67 New Zealand suffered a severe depression. By the late 1870s the Pollok Settlement was in decline. The original church was destroyed by fire in 1882 and was not rebuilt. Mr Smith struggled to serve his congregation until 1884, when he left for Auckland to help raise funds for distressed immigrant families. He died on 23 December 1888 aged 79, and was buried the next day in an unmarked pauper's grave in Waikumete cemetery.

To commemorate his endeavours and achievements, a memorial stone was unveiled at Pollok, New Zealand on 25 February 2001 in the presence of 400 descendants of the original settlers and their friends. This was funded by members of Pollokshaws Parish Church, Glasgow; the Pollokshaws Heritage Group; and Mrs Margaret Gow, a descendant of Nathaniel C. Gow, first President of the Pollok Settlement Council.

Anne Loudon

Pollok Settlement
October 8th 1925.

My Dear Anna,

How delighted I was to get your ever welcome letter the other day. Such nice homely letters you write and such lovely writing you do. I envy it. Yes I am fairly busy all day, but still I would rather be too busy than have nothing to do. I often say I would like to go to work, but Mum says she cannot do without me so. that is an end to it. We have the telephone and Post Office for Pollok Settlement, so Mother's time is always broken. We have three little children from the Orphan Home boarding with us. so that keeps me imployed. I do not mind that as I love children. I say little children, the youngest one is almost five, and the eldest one is ten. They go to school and come home for their dinner every day.

Cogan Street looking north-west to its junction with Shawbridge Street at Maxwell Cross, 1957, with Maida Street in the distance. Cogan Street was named after the Cogan family who established the Auldfield weaving mills in 1851. The projecting sign on the extreme right is a factor's advert for a vacant house, a common sight in the days of the old open closes. These signs, with details of the let on offer and the factor's name and address, were made of plywood roughly shaped like a hand with a pointing finger, and held in position high up by the 'finger' with a baulk of timber wedged across the closemouth. Another permanent sign, printed on a bill pasted high up at every tenement closemouth, had the legend 'Burst pipes & flooding, in emergency please contact ____', and gave a local plumber's name, address and phone number. The style of the discretionary road sign in the centre, reading SLOW – MAJOR ROAD AHEAD, was ultimately found to be too ambiguous and was done away with because people's interpretation of SLOW varied somewhat. In a location such as this it should have been the mandatory sign reading HALT – AT MAJOR ROAD AHEAD.

Situated adjacent to the Shaw Bridge and close to the site of the mill built by a Maxwell Laird in the sixteenth century, this triangle of grass and trees was the communal 'shilling' ground provided by him for farmers for the winnowing of their grain. When the Orange Lodge was displaced from its hall in Pollokshaws Road by road-widening later in the 1960s, it took over the Unionist Rooms – the white building behind the trees – seen here in 1961. The higher building behind is reputed to be a former miller's house and may date from the mid to late 1700s. Behind the wall in the right background is the Glasgow Corporation Cleansing Department's depot, with superintendent Mr McAdam's house visible; this and the associated buildings were all demolished in the late 1980s. Despite there having clearly been a roadway here giving access to various manufacturing and other premises, as well as to the cleansing department, the lane doesn't appear to have ever had a name. Maps old and new show it, but the occupants all appear to have Shawbridge Street addresses. Overlooking the river and barely visible on the left of this picture is a low stone wall which borders the river embankment and is probably the continuation of the original bridge parapet of 1654. Behind the telephone box is an isolated extension of John McDonald's works; this location on the banks of the River Cart was used to test the turbines they manufactured from 1907.

The old Shaw Bridge, 1934. Here buildings on the left of the picture have been demolished to allow work to begin to rebuild and widen the bridge. In the background are: the Burgh Halls partly hidden behind the Orchard Place tenement in Bengal Street; the Sir John Maxwell School, obscured by the Salvation Army Hall; and the Palladium/Pollok cinema, on the right. This view was taken from the shilling ground of the meal mill, probably at the same time as the picture on page 31 to record the scene before the changes took place.

Opened by James Graham in 1921 and originally called the Maxwell, the cinema at 99–103 Shawbridge Street had seating for 980. In 1932 Graham leased it to J. Boe who renamed it the Palladium, but Boe gave up the lease and the cinema closed in 1934. James Graham then reopened it, but later sold it to a Miss Annie M. Burns, for whom it was managed by a Mr Sagan, who again renamed it, this time as the Pollok. The cinema went by this name until final closure in 1958. In 1961/62, shortly after this picture was taken, it was demolished. I was never in it but remember hearing tales of its reputation as a flea-pit! There were stories told of the 'thrupenny rush', when children crowded into the matinee for three old pence on Saturday afternoons. Barely glimpsed behind the tree on the right is a villa in Riverbank Street believed to have belonged to another provost, while in the left background is the witch's hat tower of the old St Conval's Infants' School. The bridge parapet on the right overlooks the weir. Nettie Wren, who took many of the pictures reproduced in this book, lived 'one up' at No. 93, the tenement adjacent to the cinema, where her bedroom wall was next to that of the cinema. As a child she remembers being kept awake by the soundtrack until the program ended.

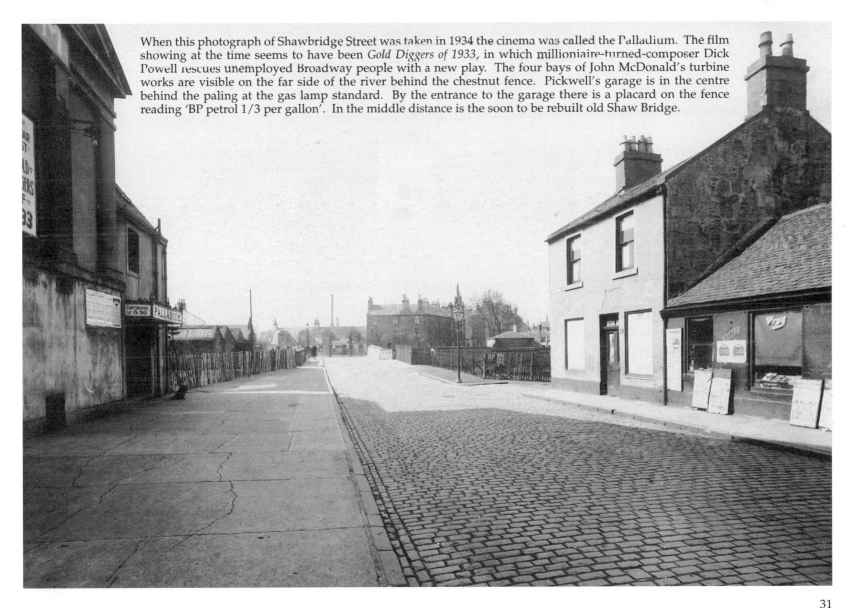

When this photograph of Shawbridge Street was taken in 1934 the cinema was called the Palladium. The film showing at the time seems to have been *Gold Diggers of 1933*, in which millionaire-turned-composer Dick Powell rescues unemployed Broadway people with a new play. The four bays of John McDonald's turbine works are visible on the far side of the river behind the chestnut fence. Pickwell's garage is in the centre behind the paling at the gas lamp standard. By the entrance to the garage there is a placard on the fence reading 'BP petrol 1/3 per gallon'. In the middle distance is the soon to be rebuilt old Shaw Bridge.

Staff of the drapery, footwear and hardware departments of Pollokshaws Co-operative Society, photographed on 17 May 1950.
Back row: Sadie Lavery, Jenny Anderson, Flora Leadbetter, Ina Irving, Netta McKay, Society Manager John Terris, Agnes Doyle, Jenny Shaw, Jean Bruce, Eva Berney.
Front row: Mary Charles, Tom McGhee (hardware manager), Helen Sutherland, Mr Lawrie (drapery manager), Rena Bryden, John Ward (who may have been drapery under manager), Margaret Meiklejohn.

Walker's ham store, left foreground, moved here from premises in Pollokshaws Road opposite Afton Terrace. Later the business had to move again, to Cogan Road, as further clearances caught up with the business. The Orchard Place tenement in Bengal Street is visible above the ham store roof, with the Burgh Halls and the Salvation Army Hall to the right. A plume of steam can be seen rising from a locomotive waiting at Pollokshaws West 'up' home signal in the background, and the railway signal box is just visible on the extreme left of the picture. Sir John Maxwell School is to the right. The building with rooflights in front of it contained a billiards hall for a time, and before demolition was used by the Giffnock Theatre Players. Like the picture on page 30, this view was also taken from the window of 93 Shawbridge Street.

Shawbridge Street seen from Kirk Lane in 1961. The fine Co-op tenement beyond the Maxwell Arms pub, set back about ten feet further from the street, had six shops at street level. These were the original Central Premises of the Pollokshaws Co-operative Society Ltd., the offices of which lay to the rear with an entrance in Christian Street. The shops were: furnishing and hardware (out of sight behind the pub); dairy (after which there was a pend giving access to a store at the rear); grocery; butcher; drapery; and footwear. In the mid-1950s I worked in the grocery, and here met my future wife who was a cash girl at the busy cash desk in the drapery. We later lived on one of the lower floors in the multi-storey flat at 124 Shawbridge Street, built six years after this picture was taken at the corner of Bengal Street on the left where the lamp-post stands. The Co-op drapery and footwear shops had an innovative method for handling cash payments which saved the assistants from trekking to the cash desk after each sale. The system consisted of twin tubes through which cartridges were propelled by vacuum. Flaps allowing the cartridges to be inserted into the tubes and a 'catching' basket were situated at various points round the premises. The sales slip and cash was placed inside one of the cartridges, which was then fed into the 'inward bound' tube. After the flap was closed it was whisked within about two seconds to the cashier, to be returned – transaction completed – via the other tube. A memorable feature of the system was constant sound of muffled plops indicating the arrival of a cartridge.

Crum Street, seen here in 1961, was probably named after the family of Thornliebank industrialists who originally traded as Walter Crum & Co. Ltd. On the left behind the railings is the playground of the Sir John Maxwell School, while to the right are the boundary railings of the Burgh Halls. The low building next to Orchard Place behind the gas lamp standard was constructed in 1940 by the Civil Defence for the use of Air Raid Precautions (ARP) and the Local Defence Volunteers (LDV), a name soon changed to the Home Guard. When the photograph was taken it was in use as a temporary children's clinic. Pollokshaws West station building is in the distance on the right. The car, believed to be an Austin Westminster, probably belonged to Dr Gallen, whose temporary surgery was in the flat outside which it is parked. Dr Gallen was for a time the official Celtic team doctor. The practice's previous surgery had been at 71 Shawbridge Street, but was displaced from there by the ongoing redevelopment. Crum Street no longer exists and the area in the foreground is now occupied by the Burgh Halls car park.

This winter 1968 view shows the soon to be demolished Co-op and Maxwell Arms pub buildings in Shawbridge Street, the latter at the corner of Bengal Street. At ground level the rear of the shop premises extended beyond the houses, so that the back-court drying area was a concrete railed platform at first floor level. Also behind the tenement, with an entrance in Christian Street, was the Co-op's counting house where the dividend calculations were supervised by Miss Nellie Rodden, whose brother Jimmy was manager of the main grocery store at Westwood Road. Farther behind the Co-op building there had been another three-close two-storey tenement in Bengal Place. A building in the centre of this block, probably built as a mission hall, was used at this time as a grocery store. The first Campbell library occupied a site in the left foreground, and between the closure of the old library and the opening of the new one a library service was maintained in the Burgh Halls for a couple of years. The new library, opened in 1969, is seen here under construction on the right. The multi-storeys are at 124 and 142 Shawbridge Street – the two numbers they were allocated were a recipe for confusion!

Ashtree Road, 1961. The baths and steamie are on the left, while the billboards mark the future site of the proposed Campbell Library. A wartime air-raid siren was fixed on the roof of the boiler house for the baths and steamie and was only removed in late 1992. Like all the other units, it was tested up to the 1960s at regular intervals after notices of the date and time had appeared in the press. The prefab house on the right was one of a row of three, and the white building in the background is one of the group forming Pollokshaws fire station. Although difficult to make out without seeing the picture at a greater enlargement, a steam locomotive with a train of tarpaulin-covered freight vehicles is in the background. At that time the *Radio Times* was printed by Carruthers at East Kilbride, and the rolls of newsprint were delivered weekly by a train of around a dozen waggons of the type glimpsed here. Two days later, a train of around a dozen box vans loaded with the finished product was brought down from East Kilbride and left in the west sidings. Later that day the engine of the evening pick-up goods train collected the vans and took the consignment south to England via Dumfries.

The Townshouse, with its squat Dutch-style clock tower, was built in 1803 as the meeting place of the town's original 'common council'. Ironically the construction of this splendid building meant that the community got into debt, an important factor in its subsequent application for burgh status. This postcard view of c.1910 shows the tower with a different finial to that on another card of similar vintage. Over the years extensions were added, one of which (on the left) may have been a washhouse as another view shows it with rooflights and a woman approaching with a loaded 'steamie' pram. A shop or shops with external entrances were located in parts of the old building, one of which was occupied by McClurg the fishmonger whose descendants carry on the business nearby today. The main part of the building was demolished in 1934 leaving only the tower containing the vestibule, although it is still known by locals as the Toonshoose.

Hugh McKenzie standing next to the granite drinking fountain at Wellgreen in the 1920s. This stood at the corner of Pollokshaws Road and Greenview Street. Another view from the 1950s shows the fountain still *in situ* but minus pillars and dome, propping up a different individual in a cloth cap! In an early postcard view (c.1900) the railing-enclosed Green is treeless, so the fifteen mature limes of today must have been planted soon after that date. The first two trees were lost when the Doctors Centre was built in the 1970s. A larger centre, now at the planning stage, means that four others will be lost.

Shawhill Road was a narrow road for most of its length, the narrowest part being here at the foot of the hill. However, when this photograph was taken in 1961 there was much less traffic and its narrowness didn't cause too much inconvenience, although when wet the cobbles on the slope could create difficult stopping conditions for drivers. A scout troop, probably from St Mary's RC Church (1864), is crossing Pleasance Street and heading for McArthur Street where a Standard Vanguard estate car is parked. The lane on the right, called simply Dovecote, led up to St Mary's Church hall and a hut where Hutcheson the builder, who had premises just beyond the plumbers (visible on the right), reared pigeons. The Co-op grocery received regular orders from him for sacks of corn feed for the doos! The building above the heads of the scouts was a public toilet with a compartment in the centre at the back containing a public telephone. The Co-op buildings are in the background. The new Campbell library now stands where the two advertising hoardings are located.

Riverbank Street seen from Riverford Road in 1961. Previously occupied by Stewart's, manufacturers of Princess marshmallows, who moved to Thornliebank in the early 1970s, the comparatively modern building (left) was used as a store for a time by Cohen's, whose nearby factory made clothing for Marks & Spencer's. It was demolished in 1992, and the site is now occupied by LiDL's store. The lower building beyond had a large sign from its previous owner, Melvilles, reading Viking Thread Mill. The mill closed in 1969, after which it was taken over by John Horn, printers & lithographers, whose main works lay behind. Further along Riverbank Street is a villa reputed to have been the house of another provost of Pollokshaws. When it was demolished in the 1970s, part of the wall fronting the street, which included the main door – complete with the last tenant's nameplate (Mrs Munn) – was retained to a height of ten feet! It survived incongruously as the door to nowhere until LiDL took over the site. Known to locals in its latter days as the Mission Hall, the building on the right was built as the Kirk of the Associate Session in 1764, and was the first permanent church in Pollokshaws. Behind lies Kirk Lane cemetery, know as the Old Vennel burial ground (est. 1770) where a daughter of Robert Burns, Elizabeth Thomson, is buried.

This view of the bridge in Factory Street (now Riverford Road) in the early years of the twentieth century shows the original structure over the River Cart. Its modern replacement was built around the time that the Pollokshaws Road and Shawbridge Street bridges were rebuilt in the 1930s. Behind the garage, with its 'Belfast' roof, are a paper mill and the engineering premises of Stewart & McKenzie Ltd. Until the 1960s Stewart & McKenzie's works extended well out into Riverford Road, reducing its width by about a third. In the distance on the left is the tenement in Riverford Road opposite McDougal Street, and on the skyline to the right is the Shaw Hill, with the then new St Conval's Primary School visible.

This photograph was taken in 1960 during a visit by transport enthusiasts organised by the Ssottish Transport Museum Society. The shed featured started life as Newlands tram depot in 1907, but eventually became a bus garage. During the final change-over to buses between 1958 and 1960, both forms of transport operated together for over a year from the depot in uncomfortable juxtaposition, until the last tram departed in summer 1960. As a bus driver I worked from this depot from 1960 to 1974. The only time of day that the depot floor could be conveniently hosed down was between 8.30 and 9 o'clock when most vehicles were out on morning rush hour services. One Thursday, pay day, a driver anxious to be first in the queue for his wages drove into the depot a little too fast. As he steered his bus into one of the lyes it skidded on the wet floor, hitting one of the hollow cast-iron poles that held the roof up. The section of roof above collapsed and the heavy beams dropped onto the bus roof, squashing its upper deck to seat level. As the collision had caused a number of bolts in adjoining parts of the roof to shear off the situation was quite serious, and the damaged bus was left holding up the roof for three weeks before engineers could work out how to carry out repairs safely. The buses in the picture are both Daimlers with Alexander bodies; D236 (SGD 219) was new in 1959; D194 (SGD 178) was new in 1958. The tram is Standard No. 1040.

Coustonhill Street, 1961, with Pleasance Street leading off to the left and Coustonholm Road to the right. This view looks up the slope of the Shaw Hill to Tracy Street. Behind the van at the top of the hill is a post-war prefabricated house, one of a number here, while the low tenements visible in the background are in Shawhill Road. David Barbour opened a large factory, the Renfield Weaving Works, in premises to the right c.1891. The old multi-bayed buildings of the works, with rooflights designed to allow north light into the building, could still be seen at this time. Buildings designed along these lines were a common feature in sectors such as the weaving industry which needed pure light to determine colours. At this point, where the single-track tramline curved round into Coustonholm Road and became double, there used to be a junction which turned off the track towards a large doorway in a factory building on the right. Research has revealed that this building was the first tram depot (during the horse-drawn era of course), dating from the 1880s. It was abandoned when Newlands depot was opened in 1907. The four Birness multi-storey flats, built 1968, now occupy this part of the Shaw Hill.

Rossendale Road, 1961. The tenements on the left formed part of a block bounded by Greenview Street, Rossendale Road, Leckie Street and Pollokshaws Road, with further tenements within the central courtyard area. This arrangement gave delivery men unfamiliar with the layout endless trouble finding addresses. In the background of this picture is Leckie Street and the old Pollokshaws East Free Presbyterian Church (1871) which closed in 1930. In that year its congregation merged with that of Pollokshaws Parish Church, which became Auldfield Parish Church, although the building seen here survived until the 1960s. During the war, on May 5/6 1941, a bomb landed in the back court behind the Bank building in Greenview Street (to the left in this view), although fortunately it did not explode. This was confirmed by Mrs Cathy Baxter (née Kelly), now of Australia, who at the time was living in a house in the backlands adjacent to where the bomb landed. She said that the area was sealed off for about a week, but she never found out what had happened at the time. She realises now that if the device had exploded she, her family and many others would have been killed.

Greenview Street, seen here in 1961, was previously called Pollok Street and before that, in the 1800s, Cowloan. In the background is Pollokshaws railway goods yard and the low office building of Vernall & Sons coal merchants. The tall tenement is the Bank building with the Wellgreen trees opposite, while the street leading off on the right is Rossendale Road. In the course of this area being cleared during redevelopment, I saw the single-storey house in the foreground being demolished by the simple expedient of having a steel cable wrapped round it and the ends attached to a bulldozer. When it was driven forward the cable cut through the stone like cheese, and the building collapsed into a pile of rubble. It is believed to have been the first police office in Pollokshaws (1860s), and on the 1913 OS map it is marked as 'police barracks'. The tarmacked area in the middle of the street shows where the single line tram rails have been removed. At one time nearly all the roads in the town had cobbled surfaces, particularly where the trams ran.

POLLOK STREET, POLLOKSHAWS.

Lower Greenview Street, *c.*1910. The base of the flagpole seen high up on the Bank building (built by the Commercial Bank of Scotland) is still there today. The structure built against its gable contains the chimney flues from the adjoining lower building. These were led into the wall of their taller neighbour and carried up to the chimneyhead above, from where smoke from the fires of the older, lower building could be directed away from the windows of the upper houses. Note the 'white' tram in the background near the Townshouse. Prior to 1935, before the advent of the Coronation and Cunarder trams, city routes were colour-coded. Wherever possible vehicles on a particular route had a broad band painted all round them between the decks in either blue, green, yellow, red or white. This system allowed intending passengers to pick out a tram from a distance that might be on the service they were waiting for, and was particularly useful on busy parts of the network such as Argyle Street in the city centre.

Leckie Street. Seen today from a viewpoint in Parkhill Road, modern Leckie Street (formerly College Street) looks very different from its appearance here. At the bottom of the steeper section is the Rossendale Road junction, with Pollokshaws Road at the far end of the street. The villa on the right, in Rossendale Road, and the segment of tenement seen alongside the church, have survived but everything else in view – with the exception of the buildings in the far background – has either gone or is hidden by new construction. Above the right-hand end of the roof ridge of the church stands a villa on the highest part of North Hill (a name seemingly lost today) in either Mannering Road or Ravenshall Road. The sun shines through a gap in the tenement on the left beyond Rossendale Road where No. 16 has already been demolished.

The following three more recent views were taken from vantage points in the high flats. This one looks west from the fourteenth floor of No. 232 Shawbridge Street in 1968. Centre left is the spire of Eastwood Parish Church, while below it and nearer the centre of the picture is Auldhouse Cottage, situated next to Auldhouse Bridge. When the photograph was taken the cottage was the residence of the director of Glasgow Corporation Parks Department, Mr Garside. The tenements of Auldhouse Avenue stand out in the middle distance near the centre. The tower block on the right was the first building of the new order in Pollokshaws.

Another view from 232 Shawbridge Street, 1968. Here the present Pollokshaws Parish Church (the United Original Secession Church of 1843) is prominent in its much-altered setting, with part of the police station roof visible in the right foreground. In the background is R. & H. Kennedy's creamery in Cogan Street with a lorry standing at the loading bay.

In this 1967 view modern Pollokshaws continues to take shape. Taken from the nineteen-storey block at 215 Shawbridge Street, it shows the 22-storey building at 142 Shawbridge Street rising with the help of the crane behind No. 160 Shawbridge Street. Beyond is the newly finished and occupied building at 124. The building at the lower left is in Shawholm Crescent. In front of the Burgh Halls is the wartime civil defence building and an area that was formerly the site of Pickwell's orchard; next to these is the two-close tenement in Bengal Street known as Orchard Place. Above Orchard Place, the newly completed Wellgreen Court can be seen. The railway goods yard with trains of waggons in the west sidings lies behind the tower of the Burgh Halls.

The gable wall collapse at Orchard Place (seen here in 1968) was due to the great storm of 15 January when the wind-speed reached hurricane force. Fortunately the building was empty and due for demolition. The low building behind the group of boys (no doubt builders of the tree house on the right), formerly the ARP post and subsequently a clinic, was also removed at this time. Note the Salvation Army hall in front of the multi at 124 Shawbridge Street, first let in April 1967. The tenement visible between Orchard Place and the hall is the Co-op building which was demolished a year or two later. Behind the school, with a construction crane seemingly sprouting from a chimney head, one of the Birness multi-storey buildings nears completion.